AUGUSTUS JOHN PAPERS
AT
THE NATIONAL LIBRARY OF WALES

CERIDWEN LLOYD-MORGAN

Aberystwyth
The National Library of Wales
1996

© Text: Ceridwen Lloyd-Morgan

© Illustrations: The National Library of Wales, reproduced by kind permission of the copyright holders, Mr Julius White and Miss Rebecca John.

ISBN: 0-907158-94-3

Cover illustration: Augustus John, self-portrait sketch (NLW MS 22777D, f.151^v).

Printed at The National Library of Wales
1996

AUGUSTUS JOHN PAPERS AT THE NATIONAL LIBRARY OF WALES

THIRTY-FIVE years after his death in 1961 Augustus John remains one of the best known Welsh-born artists, both within Wales and beyond, although this may have as much to do with his reputation as a bohemian character as with any informed appreciation of his artistic achievements. Since his death his status as an artist may have fallen as that of his sister, Gwen John, has risen — just as he himself had predicted — but public interest in him has persisted. His wide circle of friends, patrons and acquaintances brought him into contact with many of the major artistic, literary and public figures of his day, so that his story is entwined with theirs and the documentation of his life provides a window onto many areas of the cultural and even the political life of twentieth-century Britain.

The National Library of Wales began collecting archive material relating to him shortly after his death, and has continued to do so ever since. The present essay, complementing that already published on the papers of Gwen John[1] is intended to provide an introduction to the Library's holdings of Augustus John papers and to suggest some of the areas which they can illuminate. Since the artist's life and work have been amply documented elsewhere, there will be no need to provide basic biographical details here.[2]

It should be stressed at the outset that the Augustus John papers, like any other personal archive, provide only a partial view, and cannot claim to be a full or fair cross-section. As usual, a number of factors have influenced the survival of some papers rather than others. The fact that he achieved prominence as an artist and bohemian figure when still young probably helped to ensure that many of his friends, relatives and acquaintances kept with particular care the letters they received from him, and by the time he died in 1961 at the age of eighty-seven there was public awareness of the importance of preserving the personal papers of the famous. There could be no stronger contrast than the case of J. D. Innes who died at the age of twenty-seven in 1914: not only did Innes die young, but he died when the public was more concerned with the outbreak of the First World War than with collecting an artist's papers, and it is not surprising that no major archive of his has survived.

Nonetheless, large as the Augustus John archive may be, much was lost or deliberately destroyed during his own lifetime. It is not surprising that the greater bulk of the papers are from the latter part of his career, as many of these have probably been kept passively rather than for any particular reason. The very earliest letters, on the other hand, seem to have been preserved carefully and deliberately, usually because they documented events which the protagonists felt at the time were important and significant. Examples include the letters from Ida Nettleship and Gwen John and those from Augustus to Dorelia which document critical stages in the development of their relationships (see below pp. 5-7, 24-5). Similarly, close friends of Augustus, such as Michel Salaman and Ursula Tyrwhitt, clearly treasured his letters and preserved them carefully. The fact that Augustus was a lively letter-writer, often adding amusing sketches, was no doubt a further consideration.

Augustus, however, was not always as careful with their letters to him, although to some extent this may be a consequence of his peripatetic life in the early decades of the century, which also included periods spent abroad, when it may not have been so convenient to keep letters he received. Whilst Dorelia, Michel Salaman and Ursula Tyrwhitt, living more settled lives, seem to have kept most of the letters they received from him, only eight letters from Dorelia (NLW MS 22783D, ff. 110-23, [1907-?1938]) and none from the other two are among the papers in John's possession at his death. It is still comparatively unusual to find that both sides of a correspondence have been kept, although material is still coming to light. In 1995, for example, the National Library acquired ten letters from Augustus John to the composer Josef Holbrooke (now NLW MS 23410C, [1912]-43), complementing the four letters from Holbrooke to John already in its possession (NLW MS 22781D, ff. 116-19^v).

One of the National Library's first major acquisition of Augustus John papers, including the very earliest letters from him, are those which he wrote to Ursula Tyrwhitt (NLW MS 19645C), with whom he formed a close friendship during his first year as a student at the Slade and who was later to become a lifelong friend of his sister, Gwen. Ursula's letters to Augustus do not seem to have survived, but the earliest of his letters to her were written in 1895, when he was back at home in Tenby during the summer holiday, and recovering from the famous 'knock on the head'.[3] These letters were clearly written to amuse and are illustrated with lively pen and ink sketches which nicely complement the written style. 'The worst part of it is the beef tea', he complained to Ursula during his recuperation from his head injury. 'I am not allowed to remain long in peace without the slavey bearing in an enormous cup of that beverage', adding a drawing of himself, bandaged and depressed, approached by a maid bearing a steaming cup (NLW MS 19645C, item 2).

Another early group of letters are those from John to his friend Michel Salaman, another of his contemporaries at the Slade School of Art (NLW MS 14928D). This group comprises over seventy letters, written over the years 1898-1955, and thus spanning the greater part of the artist's adult life, from his later student days to his old age. However, only a few of these letters postdate 1912, and it is the earliest ones, from the period when the two young men were in most frequent contact with each other, which are the most informative. Like those to Ursula Tyrwhitt, these letters are often illustrated with sketches to entertain the recipient (see Plate I).

If the letters to Slade friends such as Ursula Tyrwhitt and Michel Salaman provide valuable evidence for the artist's life as a student, those addressed to John Sampson take us into the next phase of his life (NLW MS 21489E). In 1901, shortly after his marriage to Ida Nettleship, Augustus John moved to Liverpool to take up a post as art instructor and soon came to know Sampson, the librarian of Liverpool University and an authority on gypsies. The thirty-seven surviving letters from Augustus John to Sampson, many of them in Romani, date from 1902-27, and thus reflect their friendship almost from the beginning. They also include (f. 99) what appears to be a fairly early sketch of Sampson by John, which Dorelia McNeill sent to Dora Yates after the artist's death (see Plate II). The later acquisition by the Library of facsimile copies of Sampson's letters to Augustus (1904-30, part of the main Augustus John archive and now NLW MS 22785D, ff. 3-43) allows us to read both sides of their correspondence and glimpse something of the nature of their relationship.[4] Although the earlier letters suggest an element of hero-worship on John's side, the friendship was clearly close enough that he was able to confide in Sampson about his adulterous love for Dorelia, the use of the Romani language ensuring greater secrecy.[5] Sampson appears also to have shared with Augustus a taste for erotic and satirical versifying, for in a letter dated 1904 he mentions having written 'a few indecent songs lately, for my own amusement' (NLW MS 22785D, f. 4), and Augustus enclosed some examples of his own manufacture with his letters to Sampson (NLW MS 21459E, ff. 66-83); further examples are found in John's personal archive (e.g. NLW MS 22796E, ff. 89-90).

A number of series of letters to various correspondents were acquired piecemeal by the Library from the 1960s onwards as opportunity arose, but it was the purchase by the Library of the major archive of Gwen John Papers in 1985 and 1986 which marked a turning point. The Gwen John archive naturally contains much material relating to Augustus. Apart from the few surviving letters to Gwen from Augustus, it includes an important sequence of letters from him to his son Edwin, Gwen's executor and legatee, mostly relating to the disposal of her estate after her death. But apart from such holograph items, the archive provides much valuable information about Augustus and especially his relationship to his artist sister in the references found in surviving draft letters from Gwen to others, some of her personal notes and remarks in letters to her from relatives and friends.[6] However, the acquisition of the Gwen John Papers also made more widely known the National Library's interest in acquiring material relating to the John family. Shortly after Gwen John's archive was purchased, the Library was approached by a representative of the then owner of the main archive of Augustus John's papers. This group, which comprised papers in the artist's possession at his death, had been sold by auction on behalf of the John family at Sotheby's in London in December 1979. The National Library had been the underbidder at this sale, and was contacted shortly afterwards by an agent acting on behalf of the anonymous buyer. Negotiations for a private sale began but were suddenly suspended; eventually word began to circulate that the archive had been exported illegally to the United States. The news that the National Library had purchased the Gwen John Papers stimulated a fresh approach by the owner of Augustus's archive and in 1988 its private sale to the Library by Sotheby's was concluded. This group, together with a few complementary groups of correspondence and prose drafts, purchased from Sotheby's in 1989 and incorporated into the main archive, is calendared in the Library's *Catalogue of Augustus John Papers* (1991), together with a group of papers relating to the artist's first wife, Ida Nettleship, acquired separately in 1988.[7] A list of other Augustus John papers at the Library, superseding that provided in the *Catalogue*, is given in an appendix below, pp.33-4, together with a summary of the content of the main archive.

Throughout his adult life Augustus John corresponded regularly not only with his immediate family and friends but also with a very wide range of acquaintances. His total letter-writing output is enormous and it is not surprising, therefore, that many other institutions have important holdings of his correspondence. His letters to George Bernard Shaw, Marie Stopes and others are held at the British Library, for example, whilst his letters to Chaloner and Mary Dowdall are at the Liverpool Record Office. Other groups are held in collections abroad, those to William Rothenstein, for instance, in the Houghton Library of Harvard University, and those to Bertrand Russell at McMaster University, Canada.[8] Nonetheless, the National Library's holdings can be regarded as the most extensive single archive of Augustus John's written papers, paralleling the substantial collection of visual material held at the Library's sister institution, the National Museum of Wales in Cardiff.[9] Although the Department of Pictures and Maps at the National Library has also acquired over the years a number of important drawings and paintings by Augustus John, including a sketch by him of Gwen John and a portrait in oils of David Lloyd George,[10] it should not be forgotten that the manuscript archive too includes sketches and drawings. Augustus John's habit, in his student days and early adulthood, of adding sketches to his letters to close friends such as Michel Salaman and Ursula Tyrwhitt, has already been mentioned. Such sketches are mostly of himself — unshaven, bandaged and gloomily drinking beer (NLW MS 19645C, item 5, [summer 1895], Plate III) for example, or slouching by a tent, campfire and donkey whilst camping with Ambrose McEvoy at Newgale in Pembrokeshire (*ibid*. item 3, see Plate IV), or, more cheerfully, in a café in France, again with McEvoy, watching 'a young lady exquisitely beautiful attired as a soldier' singing on a small stage 'songs of dubious meaning' (*ibid*., item 7, 1900, Plate V). However, he sometimes includes sketches of mutual friends and acquaintances, such as his sequence of comic drawings of Wilson Steer's long beard (*ibid*., items 2, 5, Plate VI), or the sketch of Gwen John in her finery astounding Brown and Tonks at the Slade (*ibid*. item 6). Similar illustrations are found in the long series of letters he wrote to Dorelia McNeill, especially those written during his urgent second courtship of her whilst she was in France with Gwen John and later in Bruges with a young Belgian artist, as well as in the early years of their relationship after her return to England (NLW MS 22776D, ff. 31-51 *passim*, Plate VII). After the death of his first wife, Ida Nettleship, in 1907, Dorelia became established as Augustus John's second wife and the letters that he wrote to her whilst travelling or undertaking commissions away from home continue to be illustrated by sketches of himself, of sights he had seen (such as the people of Genoa), or of the pictures he was painting, including the controversial portrait of Harold Chaloner Dowdall in all his finery as Lord Mayor of Liverpool (NLW MSS 22776D, ff. 88-109^v *passim*, 120, 127^v, 140, 147^v, 148^v, see Plates VIII-X).

Apart from such incidental drawings, whose chief purpose was to amuse the recipient of the letters, the main archive also includes four sketchbooks containing rough drawings, mainly of people, in pencil and in ink. The earliest of these (NLW MS 22791C) dates from 1908, when the artist was staying at Diélette, and includes sketches of single figures and a design for a figure composition typical of that period (f. 6).[11] The other three sketchbooks (NLW MSS 22792-4A) are from the mid 1920s, one of them being inscribed 'Villa Ste Anne, Martigues'.

Nonetheless, it is not only the sketchbooks and incidental drawings in letters which document Augustus John's activity as an artist. His correspondence often records offers of commissions, accounts of sittings for portraits and his own and other people's reactions to finished work. It was only in artistic terms that he was able to express his grief at the death of his wife Ida in March 1907, when, writing to his mother-in-law, Ada Nettleship, he laments that he had 'never painted her', meaning that in his paintings and drawings of her he had not done justice to her. He was 'counting on doing the real thing in the end — she was such a big subject', he reflected (NLW MS 22775C, f. 69^v). The letters he sent to Dorelia during his absences from home provide a useful commentary on his work, even at times an almost daily account of his activities (NLW MSS 22776-8), but in later life, when his relationship with at least some of his sons had improved, he occasionally included news of his painting in letters to them, notably those to Sir Caspar John (NLW MS 22775C, ff. 2-55^v, 1950-61). Although in the earliest period of his relationship with Dorelia his letters are more concerned with wooing her and with the need to establish a *modus vivendi* between them and Ida, once their situation was more settled and he felt sure of Dorelia, he begins to mention his painting; the focus moves away from an obsessive concern to ensure her continued presence in his life, and returns to his work. In fact, although the letters to Dorelia are the nearest source we have to a diary of Augustus John, his main concern in them, once he has won her, seems to be first to keep her and please her, and then to reassure her that he is working hard and generally behaving himself — in short telling her what he thinks she ought to hear or what she would wish to hear. At first he mentions his progress with portraits of Dorelia herself (e.g. NLW MS 22776D, f. 50, ?late summer, 1905), but as time goes on he reports on his work in general, boasting in 1907, for example, that he is doing 'lovely painting', or preparing a 'vast cartoon' or that his pictures are selling well, as when he reports selling £225 worth on the first morning of an exhibition, probably at the Carfax Gallery, in late 1907 (*ibid.*, ff. 58^v, 61, 64).

As his portrait commissions increase, so do the more specific references to sitters, which can not only help to provide a chronology or indicate the length of time spent on a particular portrait but also hint at his feelings towards the sitters. In 1908 he reports that he is about to start painting Lady Ottoline Morrell (*ibid.*, f. 66^v), but seven years later he is still worrying at this subject. Writing from Galway in the autumn of 1915 he confides that it would be a good idea 'to get Ottoline's portrait from memory. She is rather awful to examine closely'. He perseveres, but finds he has no easel big enough for the full length (NLW MS 22777D, ff. 90-1). In writing to Dorelia he was able to express his frustrations and annoyances as well as his successes, often seesawing between conflicting emotions. When painting the great Celtic scholar, Professor Kuno Meyer, in Liverpool in 1911 he at first reassures her and himself that the picture is 'going to be all right' but soon it becomes the 'bloody old portrait' and finally he complains that portrait commissions are a waste of time (NLW MS 22776D, ff. 141, 143, 148). Again, writing from Berlin in 1925 he talks of the 'damned portraits' keeping him tied up but hastily adds that they will be worth doing. However, it is not always possible to judge how far such comments are a true reflection of his feelings and how far they are intended to entertain Dorelia or reassure her that he is working hard. This is especially true of his apparently frank comments, for example when he reports of the finished portrait of Gustav Stresemann that 'even his wife admits it's like him at his worst' (NLW MS 22778D, f. 68, [?April 1925])[12], or complains that the beautiful and elegant Princess Bibesco 'has the most disconcerting habits', for she insists on picking her nose during sittings. So intense was his implied disgust that in recounting this story he felt obliged to turn to French (*ibid.*, ff. 23-4, [December 1919]). Perhaps his worst contempt is reserved for his American sitters. Writing from New Hampshire in 1928 he states that although the work is progressing well the people have 'no understanding' and that he has to point out to them 'the difference between a hired photographer and a painter' (*ibid.*, f. 101).

Inevitably, the letters to Dorelia become scarcer towards the end of his life, as he travelled less, but those that survive are concerned less with his painting than with other matters, such as his health. Thus in a letter sent from Paris in August 1950 he reports in detail on a course of injections he is undergoing (*ibid.*, f. 143). The last reference to his work in this series dates from 1944, when he was staying in Cardiganshire and drawing the portrait of Miss Alicia Gower Jones, headmistress of a girls' grammar school (*ibid.*, f. 140).[13]

Apart from this substantial and often apparently frank series of letters to Dorelia, there are other groups of correspondence which help to document his work, especially the portraits. These include, most notably, his correspondence with the sitters themselves. Within the main archive, Augustus John's own *Nachlass*, naturally it is only the sitters' letters to the artist which have been preserved, although his letters to them may sometimes be available elsewhere, in the National Library or in other public collections. Not surprisingly, letters from sitters tend to reveal more about themselves than about Augustus. Those from Marie Stopes, for example, are concerned at all times with her desire to define herself as a writer and therefore a fellow creative artist (NLW MS 22785D, ff. 132-4, 1948-56). The weather has been so horrible, she complains at one point, 'that I have had to sit by the fire and write a 3 act play' (*ibid.*, f. 134). Nonetheless, some correspondents express a seemingly sincere appreciation, as, for example, the rather touching letter from James Joyce, thanking the artist for the drawing of him included in a book, although the praise is tempered by Joyce's confession that his poor sight prevents him seeing it clearly: 'Praise from a purblind poet would be ridiculous', but the drawing 'is the one thing in the volume which is indiscutable'.[14] He also reminds Augustus that he had promised Nora, Joyce's wife, one of the other sketches he had made, 'the one that made her cry' (NLW MS 22782D, ff. 132-3ᵛ, March [1933]). Humphrey Sumner, Warden of All Souls College, Oxford, writing in 1950 to arrange a sitting at the behest of A. L. Rowse, uneasily prepares himself for the worst by warning Augustus that he may find it 'difficult to seize on to much in a very scrawny academic', although he hurriedly praises the artist's oil portrait of Bodley's Librarian, Edmund Craster, 'duskily gleaming with a latent Northumbrian ferocity' (NLW MS 22785D, f. 159ᵛ). Sumner's reaction to his own portrait is not recorded but Rowse confidently assured Augustus that it was 'as fine a thing as you have ever done' (NLW MS 22784D, f. 148ᵛ)[15].

Although in many instances the letters to Dorelia suggest that Augustus was glad to put many of the commissioned portraits behind him, sometimes clear evidence emerges of a rapport and even of a friendship developing between artist and sitter. T. E. Lawrence (Lawrence of Arabia) is perhaps the best example, and in this instance the National Library was able to acquire both sides of the correspondence, which gives a fuller, more balanced view of the relationship than is usually possible (NLW MSS 22775C, ff. 58-65, 22783D, ff. 5-13). Both men appear to have understood that they both normally presented a particular persona to the world and having recognized this, no doubt implicitly, were able to express themselves in unusually open terms. Reporting that Augustus's 'wrathful portrait' of him had been rapidly sold, Lawrence playfully boasts that although 'you will naturally think the glory is yours ... I believe it's due to the exceeding beauty of my face', and recounts his embarrassment when he was admiring one of the portraits at an exhibition and 'a person with a military moustache ... blurted out to us, "Looks a bloody sort of creature, doesn't he?" ... I looked very pink' (NLW MS 22783D, f. 6). The letters from Augustus have a similarly ironic, self-deprecating tone. In September 1919 he offers to continue a portrait of Lawrence even though, he adds in a burst of frankness, 'some of the Ta[te] Gallery people don't seem to want [it]', and in 1923 confesses with mock modesty 'I still draw a little'(NLW MS 22775C, ff. 58, 62). He even admits to Lawrence that some of his sitters are less than happy with the experience of having Augustus paint their portraits, notably an 'ex-grocer and peer' (presumably Lord Leverhulme). 'I actually frightened him into violence', he adds (*ibid.*, f. 58).

The relationship between Augustus and his agents is not so well documented by the archive. Only two letters from Jack Knewstub, dated 1911 and 1926, survive (NLW MS 22782D, ff. 165-9), although the first does refer to actual and potential customers, including the notorious Madame Strindberg, estranged wife of the dramatist, who had bought three drawings.[16] The second is more concerned with Knewstub's own health and financial problems. He utters dark warnings that if 'this enterprise of mine' comes under the control of the Bloomsbury group there will be a 'pitiable outlook' for Augustus John's investments (f. 167). Nonetheless, this letter does provide more concrete information, for it encloses a copy of a letter to the artist's solicitors, confirming that forty paintings and as many drawings have been shipped to Mitchell Kennerley of the Anderson Galleries, New York.[17] The letters of Dudley Tooth, who handled Augustus's work in the final phase of his career, are far more business-like, and full of bracing comments about framing and arrangements for collection, with discreet hints at the need to finish pictures which the artist has promised to 'push on with' (NLW MS 22786D, ff. 89-97^v, 1960-1). Curiously, only one letter from John's American patron, John Quinn survives, whereas his sister Gwen preserved some thirty-five of Quinn's letters to her.[18] Perhaps the fact that Augustus was not so financially dependent on Quinn as was Gwen, or perhaps his lack of sympathy with the American and his 'vulgar Yankee habits of expense', which irritated him when they toured France together (NLW MS 22776D, f. 156), meant that he attached smaller importance to their correspondence. The surviving letter, dated 1913, is, however, fairly typical of Quinn's style, for his eagerness to buy two pictures, 'The Mumpers' and 'Forza e Amore', from the artist is set in the context of Quinn's battle against US import duty on books and art, and he adds to his expression of delight at J. D. Innes's improved health one of his usual lectures on the role of the teeth and stomach in causing illness (NLW MS 22784D, ff. 80-4).

Of those many letters in praise of his work which Augustus received, it must surely have been those from fellow artists which gave him the greatest pleasure, for example those from the painter Matthew Smith (NLW MS 22785D, f. 83-103^v, 1930-58). Smith's wife, Gwen Salmond, had been a contemporary and close friend of Augustus, Gwen John and Ida Nettleship at the Slade, but the Smiths' marriage did not last.[19] Nevertheless, Augustus and Matthew enjoyed a long and close friendship, reflected in a series of letters from Matthew Smith to Augustus, as well as by brief references elsewhere, as in letters from Augustus's daughter Vivien John to her brother Edwin. 'Matthew Smith has painted a portrait of Daddy's stomach!' she announced delightedly in a letter dated 24 August 1944. 'I believe the chief colo[u]r is red!! Daddy has done a very pale one of M. Smith' (NLW MS 22312D, f. 161). Smith's own letters suggest much mutual respect and kindness between the two artists. In a letter dated 11 February 1930, he thanks Augustus for his comments on his painting, describing them as 'an encouragement to be grateful for' (*ibid.*, f. 84), and praises Augustus's work, as well as discussing the work of other artists such as Cézanne. 'I came away thinking, "Well, Cézanne did something akin to bursting through the sound barrier"', he reported after visiting an exhibition (*ibid.*, f. 99^v, 28 August 1956).

Augustus John's kindness to younger artists also emerges from their letters to him, notably those from Carrington, whose friendship with Dorelia and her two 'ravishing daughters', Poppet and Vivien, is reflected in surviving letters to both

Augustus and Dorelia (NLW MSS 22779E, ff. 136-8ᵛ, 22789D, ff. 3-29). These letters also refer to Carrington's visits to the John family at Fryern Court, and the decorative work she undertook for Dorelia (NLW MSS 22779E, f. 138, 22789D, f. 23).[20] The sculptress Fiore de Henriquez and the budding painter Breon O'Casey (son of the playwright Seán O'Casey) are others whose letters express gratitude for his support and encouragement (NLW MSS 22781D, f. 109, 22784D, ff. 10-11).

Correspondence with other established artists was not always conducted on such close terms of friendship, however. The single letter from Roger Fry to Augustus included in the archive is no more than a circular letter on a technical matter (NLW MS 22780E, f. 136, 1931), and the two letters from Henry Lamb, who had once been very much part of the John circle, are somewhat conventional, even distant, the second being little more than a nicely turned, albeit apparently sincere, expression of condolence on the death of Augustus John's son Henry (NLW MS 22783D, ff. 1-2, [?1907], 1935). Although a series of nine letters from William Rothenstein has survived (NLW MS 22784D, ff. 135-46), they are couched in friendly but not intimate terms. However, they do contain a few revealing comments. Rothenstein admired wholeheartedly John's early work but was confident enough — perhaps as a former contemporary at the Slade — to criticise at times, noting that an exhibition at Tooth's in 1929 was 'not worthy of your powers' (*ibid.*, f. 140). As time goes on, however, Rothenstein's letters to Augustus increasingly hark back nostalgically to the early years of their acquaintance, but they lack the warmth and apparent sincerity of his letters to Gwen John (NLW MS 22311D, ff. 1-4, 1926).

Perhaps the liveliest series of letters to John from a fellow artist are those from Wyndham Lewis, of which eighteen survive and, unusually, represent five decades, from *c.* 1904-5 to 1952, which may indicate that Augustus consciously preserved them (NLW MS 22783D, ff. 16-42ᵛ). Lewis's letters show that relations were not always smooth between him and the John *ménage*, for at one point he complains of Augustus's behaviour to him and later of doors being slammed in his face when he came visiting (*ibid.*, ff. 24ʳ⁻ᵛ, 2ᵛ, [1907, 1910]), but he does have the grace to apologize for his 'unnecessary sneers' (*ibid.*, f. 29, [1910]). Despite these tensions, however, and the rather egocentric tone of the earliest letters, both perhaps indicative of feelings of rivalry, Lewis makes no secret of his respect for John as a man and an artist, and responds in a positive and constructive way to his work. Pronouncing himself ready to support Augustus if need be, he describes John's designs for the house of Sir Hugh Lane as 'very welcome'.[21] 'Let it be an authentic earthquake', he added. 'What's the good of being an island, if you are not a *volcanic island!*' (*ibid.*, f. 32, [1910]).

That Augustus was not in any danger of being insular, volcanic or otherwise, however, is demonstrated by letters from artists outside Britain. Apart from anglophone artists such as the American William James (NLW MS 22782D, ff. 4-5) and the Canadian Yousuf Karsh (*ibid.*, f. 138), he corresponded with artists from a number of other countries, including the Mexican Diego Rivera (NLW MS 22784D, ff. 119-20), and French painters such as Paul Maze (NLW MS 22783D, f. 138) and Chantal Quenneville (NLW MS 22784D, ff. 73-9ᵛ), whilst in 1958 Modigliani's daughter, Jeanne Modigliani Nechstein, wrote to him, asking for information about his contact with her father (NLW MS 22783D, f. 184).

Apart from visual artists, Augustus came to know many of the leading writers and musicians of the day, and his papers give some idea of the wide range of his social contacts in these spheres. Writers as varied as Roy Campbell, Frank Harris, Joseph Hone, Ethel Mannin and Edith and Sacheverell Sitwell are among his many correspondents, the latter revealing a genuine interest in John's work (NLW MSS 22779E, ff. 118-25, 22781D, ff. 97-101, 123-31, 22783D, f. 130, 22785D, ff. 77-82ᵛ). Only one letter, dated 1913, survives from Lytton Strachey, an earlier admirer of John, but another four, addressed to Dorelia and written between 1913 and 1931, are included in the archive, giving a better indication of the nature and length of the friendship between Strachey and the Johns (NLW MSS 22786D, f. 139, 22789D, ff. 97-101ᵛ). His letters to Dorelia are full of amusing anecdotes and vignettes to entertain her, from Wyndham Lewis 'pursuing bonnes along the plage' at Dieppe (NLW MS 22789D, f. 97ᵛ) to his description of himself in 'the smallest [house] in Scotland ... crammed in with two young ladies, two young gentlemen and — a dog! ... As the 2 young ladies and 2 young gentlemen very naturally paired off together, I was left to solace myself with it as best I might' (*ibid.*, f. 97). Equally bantering are the three letters from George Bernard Shaw to Augustus, written in February 1944 when the latter was painting the portrait of Field Marshall Montgomery and Shaw had been present at the sittings to entertain Montgomery.[22] Shaw urges John to 'take that old petrol rag that wiped out so many portraits of me (all masterpieces) and rub out this one', before telling him exactly how he ought to depict the sitter. The next day, however, he began to suspect this was 'an ebul[l]ition of senile excitement', and wrote again, confessing that in his late eighties he can never be quite sure whether he is 'talking sense or old man's drivel' (NLW MS 22785D, ff. 62-3).

Not all of John's literary correspondents were entertaining, but the letters of even the more morose may provide useful insights into their character as well as biographical details. A series of eleven letters from Arthur Symons (NLW MS 22786D, ff. 1-21) make depressing reading, as the earliest ones date from late 1908 and 1909 when he was suffering a mental breakdown, and are pathetic in their insistence on Augustus's role as a true bohemian, a faithful friend and brother artist. They form a striking contrast to those written in 1919 and 1920, after Symons's recovery, to Gwen John, with whom his relationship was fatherly, without the hero-worshipping and yet competitive element in his feelings towards Augustus. Although Symons's ill health seems to have accelerated rather than inhibited his writing of verse, the finished examples which he sent to Augustus, written in his usual 'decadent' style, fall well below his usual standard (*ibid.*, ff. 22-65). Those in the notebook in which his amanuensis, Miss Agnes Tobin, wrote down from his dictation poems he composed during the worst period of his madness, a manuscript which somehow found its way into John's personal archive, are little more than doggerel but harrowing in their reflection of his disturbed state of mind (NLW MS 22801A).

Augustus John's lifelong love of France and its culture is reflected in his correspondence with French literary figures, for example Paul Fort, to whose review, *Vers et Prose*, the artist subscribed (NLW MS 22780E, f. 102, 1911), whilst the John family's frequent stays at St Rémy in Provence led to friendship with the local writer and pillar of Provençal culture, Marie Mauron, from whom one letter in French survives, containing vivid impressions of life in wartime France under the German occupation (NLW MS 22783D, ff. 134-6^v). She recounts how the Germans had hoped to requisition Augustus's *mas* [farmhouse], but fled in horror at the lack of electricity each time they went to inspect it.

Amongst the letters from creative artists of all kinds, it is striking how many were Welsh by birth, residence, adoption or temporary affiliation. In view of John's involvement between the wars with the Contemporary Art Society for Wales (CASW), it is not surprising to find a letter from that period from the Welsh artist Cedric Morris, who, like John, had been a founder member of the Society (NLW MS 22783D, f. 178).[23] The way in which he was drawn into such organizations in Wales, perhaps more at their instigation than his,[24] is also reflected in his correspondence with influential public and private collectors such as David Bell, curator of the Glynn Vivian Gallery in Swansea, and Mrs Winifred Coombe Tennant, an enthusiastic buyer of work by J. D. Innes and other Welsh artists, and a prominent figure in Eisteddfod circles, where she rejoiced in the bardic name 'Mam O'Nedd' [*recte* 'Mam o Nedd', 'a mother from Neath'] (NLW MS 22779E, ff. 69-70, 22786D, ff. 70-4^v).[25] It is perhaps significant, however, that Augustus John's papers contain so little evidence of any personal contact with indigenous Welsh artists (see below, pp. 18-20), although letters survive from a few painters of Welsh descent or identified as Welsh by the Welsh establishment, such as Frank Brangwyn (NLW MS 22779E, f. 90, 1947).

The same is true of writers. It is striking how few of those represented by letters to John were Welsh by birth or upbringing. Apart from Dylan Thomas, whom Augustus John first knew in London, and from whom a single begging letter survives (NLW MS 22786D, f. 77, 8 December 1950), and that other consummate self-promoter, the editor of *Wales*, Keidrych Rhys (Rhys to John, NLW MS 22784D, ff. 116-18, 1956-60, and John to Rhys, NLW MSS 22745D, f. 1, 1938, and 23419D, ff. 12-15, 1959), most of his literary acquaintances in Wales were incomers such as the novelists John Cowper Powys (Powys to John, NLW MS 22784D, ff. 65-6, 1955-6, John to Powys, NLW MS 21872D, ff. 50-1, 1958), and James Hanley (NLW MS 22781D, f. 87). But the fact that the archive contains no letters from another Wales-based but non-native writer, the novelist Richard Hughes, whom Augustus knew well, is a useful reminder of the arbitrariness of documentary survival.

Again, the musicians Josef Holbrooke and Philip Heseltine ('Peter Warlock'), who both spent long periods in Wales, were Englishmen with Welsh connnections or interests.[26] Lord Howard de Walden, who was for a time a patron of both Holbrooke and John, cut an eccentric, even alien, figure to most Welsh people, despite (or perhaps because of) his attempt to create a Welsh baronial lifestyle in Chirk Castle (which he leased), his pride in his Welsh ancestry, and his efforts to produce plays, pageants and operas inspired by Welsh mythology. Although only one letter from Howard de Walden to John is included in the archive (NLW MS 22786D, ff. 2-3), this is supplemented by a number of references in Augustus's letters to Dorelia (e.g. NLW MS 22777D, ff. 24, 25, 45^v, 46, 57, 62, 92, 117, 124, 138) many of them recording his increasingly desperate attempts to paint a portrait of Lady Howard de Walden.[27]

As his lack of a broad range of contacts within *pura Wallia* may indicate, Augustus John's feelings towards Wales and his perception of the country and its culture were extremely complex, even problematic. Although he enjoyed being accorded high status by the Welsh as one of the foremost 'Welsh artists' of his time, his attitude to his native land was ambivalent and his comments reveal a rather superficial knowledge of it. Like his sister, Gwen, Augustus often uses England and English where Britain and British would be used today, but in this he was only following common contemporary practice.[28] Judging by letters written during his early days as a Slade student, in his youth he did not perceive himself as in any way different from his English-born contemporaries. Early references to Wales in his letters from this period, written during holidays at home in Tenby, define Pembrokeshire mainly as an ideal place for a holiday, for bathing and the outdoor life. 'Today I had a "glorious" bathe in a little bay some distance away on the coast', he wrote to Michel Salaman in the summer of 1898. 'The sun tho' far away shone hot and uninterrupted by clouds which however ranged themselves exquisitely in the right place'. (NLW MS 14982D, f. 3ᵛ). His comments on Tenby are indistinguishable from those on Vattetot-sur-Mer in France, which he visited the following year (*ibid*. ff. 11-14). As well as outdoor physical activity, Pembrokeshire offered visual stimulation to the artist: 'The country looks magnificent', he enthused (letter to Michel Salaman, *ibid*., f. 5, 22 June [1898]). He saw his native country, as he did France, through the eyes of a visitor from outside, an artist-tourist in search of the picturesque. 'The country round here is quite fine', he wrote to Charles Conder from Tenby in June 1901. 'I should think you'll like it immensely' (NLW MS 23410C, f. 14). The magnificent fish-women he sees at Boulogne in 1907 and who 'must be painted' are explicitly put in the same category as the women of 'Langum' [Llangwm], near Haverfordwest, who go selling oysters 'in a peculiar costume ... I burn to go and see them' (NLW MS 22776D. f. 57). Eighteen years later he harked back to the same image, asking Dorelia to bring a postcard of Llangwm women. Making a picture of them had been on his mind for years, he wrote (NLW MS 22778D, f. 57).

Although Augustus, having once left Wales for London, chose never to return to live permanently there, he did visit his native country on a number of occasions, partly as a result of invitations from friends, would-be sitters and Welsh organizations such as the National Eisteddfod or various art societies. Moreover, his father lived on in Tenby until his death at an advanced age in 1938, necessitating duty visits from time to time. As a young man, he found these unbearably tedious, complaining to Charles Conder in 1901 that his father insists on talking about 'motor-cars and such things which tho' marvellous do not interest me', or lapses into narrating the plot of Marie Corelli's latest novel (NLW MS 23410C, ff. 14ᵛ-15). But even after his father's estate had been wound up and no further business required his presence there, in the last decade of his long life his thoughts again turned to Pembrokeshire, as he wrote to his son Caspar in 1952, the letter being dated — perhaps significantly? — 1 March, St David's Day, but his words reflect little more than the typical nostalgia of old age and they lack conviction: 'I get a nostalgia for Wales now and then, and especially the region round Prescelly — including the coast. I hope to persuade somebody to drive me down that way before long' (NLW MS 22775C, f. 5ᵛ). He seems also to have been genuinely pleased to receive the freedom of the borough of Tenby in 1959 (see e.g. NLW MSS 22783D, ff. 179-80, 22787D, f. 17). Like the artist Nina Hamnett, who was also born in Tenby but never returned permanently, he could not completely turn his back, and a letter which she sent to him from her hospital bed in London in 1955 hints that they often chatted about Tenby. She announces excitedly that she has met a nurse 'related to half Tenby', who passes on the

Tenby newspapers, and Nina even encloses a cutting for him (NLW MS 22781D, f. 84, cutting not preserved).

If, as his early letters suggest, the young Augustus did not define himself as specifically Welsh, there can be no doubt that he came to accept the label later imposed upon him and was quite prepared to wear it when convenient. He had certainly been glad to leave home, but in doing so he was escaping from his father and the suffocating respectability of middle-class Tenby rather than from Wales as a country. It was probably the same factors which drove Gwen John first to London and then to Paris, and their brother Thornton and sister Winifred to settle even further away in Canada and California respectively. As early as 1910 Winifred wrote to Gwen John that their father was worrying her to go home but that she was determined not to return (NLW MS 22307C, f. 123). Augustus was thus the only one of the four to remain in Britain, despite his frequent travels, and to maintain any regular contact with Wales and Welsh people. The reasons for this are probably complex, but one factor was probably his early achievement of fame and success as an artist, among the Welsh as well as the English. And if being defined as a Welshman were to bring him and his work to greater prominence, he was apparently prepared to accept success on those terms.

But even at the start of his career, before his adoption by the Welsh establishment as a symbol of Welsh success, Augustus had already found himself defined as Welsh by others and had even come to think of himself in those terms. The major turning point in this respect was almost certainly his meeting John Sampson, who brought him into closer contact with Welsh life. Augustus took up his teaching post in Liverpool in 1901 and in a letter to her mother in August or early September that year, Ida mentions that she and Augustus have been invited to stay with the Sampsons for the first week or two of the new term. 'They are delightful people', she reports, and describes John Sampson, significantly, as 'a student of Welsh and Romani' (NLW MS 22798B, f. 35^{r-v}). It is likely that Sampson as an Englishman took it for granted when they first met that Augustus, born and bred in Wales, would define himself as a Welshman, especially since Sampson's familiarity with Welsh people, both in North Wales itself and in the vast Liverpudlian Welsh community, was probably confined to Welsh-speaking Northerners with a stronger sense of their Welsh identity than that possessed by south Pembrokeshire people.

The correspondence between John and Sampson contains frequent references to their travels in North Wales in search of the gypsies. As early as April 1902 Augustus mentioned spending 'three happy days in Wales with Sampson' in a letter to Michel Salaman (NLW MS 14928D, f. 54^v). It was Sampson who introduced to Augustus a new, more attractive image of Wales. Instead of the anglicised, respectable, pious, middle-class Wales of Tenby, on his trips with Sampson to Betws Gwerful Goch near Corwen he discovered a very different and far more enticing Wales, peopled with colourful characters speaking Welsh and Romani, a world full of singing, dancing, storytelling, swearing and fisticuffs. Sampson himself summed it up in similar terms when he described his completed book on *The Dialect of the Gypsies of Wales* as 'a complete guide to sorcery, fortune-telling, love and courtship, kichimas [inns], fiddling, harping, poaching and the life of the road generally' (NLW MS 22785D, f. 22, letter dated 21 November 1919).[29]

When John's first son, David, was born in Liverpool, it appears to have been this new consciousness of a Welsh identity which led him to the choice of name, and he even began to take Welsh lessons, as Ida reported to her sister-in-law, Winifred John in July 1902 (NLW MS 22311D, ff. 139^{r-v}). Again in 1905, while staying in Liverpool, Augustus refers in a letter to Dorelia to a Miss Owen resuming her teaching of Welsh to him (NLW MS 22776D, f. 45); perhaps it was she who had taught him three years earlier. The language would not have been completely new to him, however, for he was exposed to it to some extent as a child, since there were Welsh speakers even amongst the anglophone 'down belows' of south Pembrokeshire. Not only did the John children's own grandfather speak Welsh[30], but they had a nurse who came from Preseli and would therefore be Welsh-speaking, and they even visited her home.[31] This is doubtless why Ida, in her letter referring to Welsh lessons, had no need to gloss the final message: 'Gussie says — Yr wyf yn ysgrifenu i chwi' [I am writing to you]. Augustus clearly expected Winifred to understand at least a simple sentence in Welsh (NLW MS 22311D, f. 139^v). Augustus John's rapid mastery of Romani under Sampson's tutelage indicates that, unlike his sister Gwen, he had a good ear and picked up languages without difficulty or inhibition. His knowledge of Welsh, however, does not seem to approach that of his Romani, and his interest in Welsh may reflect little more than an interest in languages in general: it was fascinating as a language and, like his French or Spanish, could be useful while travelling. He may well have acquired sufficient tourist Welsh to communicate easily with landlords and shopkeepers in Merionethshire and Denbighshire, where English was not universally spoken in the early twentieth century, and he doubtless found some command of Welsh a useful asset in ingratiating himself with young women. This was certainly an image which appealed to him, even at the end of his life. As late as May 1961 he boasted to his son Caspar that 'a personable young Welsh woman' had offered him the use of her flat, adding suggestively: 'I am keen to improve my *Welsh*' (NLW MS 22775C, f. 53^v). For his grasp of written Welsh there is even less evidence, but judging by the notes in

Welsh he scribbled on the back of a letter received from Lytton Strachey in 1913, he seems to have relied more on his ear than on any formal study of Welsh grammar and orthography.[32]

His enthusiasm for North Wales may have been first kindled by John Sampson, but was undoubtedly fuelled by another Welshman, J. D. Innes.[33] Because Innes, born in Llanelli in 1887, had gone to school in Brecon and then studied at Carmarthen Art School in 1904-5, he had had a far greater experience of Wales and Welsh life than Augustus, whose childhood in a more anglicised district had been followed by boarding school in England before he went to the Slade. Innes moved on from Carmarthen to the Slade in 1906 and probably first met Augustus in 1907. It was in 1910 that Innes first went on a painting tour of North Wales and in May of the following year he persuaded John, now a close friend, to accompany him on a similar trip. The difference in their attitudes to Wales is summed up by a wistful letter from Innes, written in August 1913 when he was exiled in Tavistock, nursing his advanced tuberculosis: 'I wish I was in Wales. Since I left it I find myself to be very much a Welshman and would like to be back' (NLW MS 22781D, f. 143). If Augustus John's perception of his own Welshness seems to have been largely imposed on him predefined, in Innes's case the definition of himself as Welsh seems, by contrast, to have come from within himself.

Despite the fact that John's reputation for drinking and womanising would scarcely endear him to large sections of the population of Wales before the Second World War, there existed in the Welsh establishment a persistent eagerness to find figures of Welsh origin who had succeeded in England and whose success could be exploited to the supposed advantage of Wales. As in the case of David Lloyd George, Augustus John's older contemporary, the shortcomings of the man's private life were conveniently overlooked while concentrating on public achievements in the English sphere. Even clergymen were amongst those anxious to remind the artist of his Welsh connections, as witness his reply to a letter from the Reverend R. J. Jones of Cardiff.[34] Art societies were naturally keen to claim him as a compatriot. In 1930, for example, the South Wales Art Society optimistically invited John to become an honorary member of the Society and to exhibit a picture in their next annual exhibition. With a disarming flash of honesty the Secretary reveals the true motive: to have one of his pictures in their show would ensure better press coverage (NLW MS 22785D, f. 114). Similarly in 1933 he was proposed as President of the Royal Cambrian Academy, perhaps in an attempt to raise the Academy's profile, and certainly on rather shaky grounds, judging by the letter to Augustus from John Littlejohns, reporting on a meeting with — significantly — the *London* members of the Academy. Littlejohns quotes a letter he has sent to Sir Cuthbert Grundy stating that members were impressed by Augustus John's interest in the RCA and his 'ideas for making it a very important factor in Welsh national life'. Because of his 'personal distinction, his sympathy with, and understanding of Welsh opinion and sentiment, and his social influence among leading Welshmen' [sic], Augustus was 'more likely than any other artist to change the present national attitude of unconcern with the RCA into one of active beneficial interest' (NLW MS 22783D, f. 50). This statement is so disingenuous that it may have given the artist as much cause for laughter as for pride.

His relationship with the National Eisteddfod, then the ultimate expression of Welsh culture and nationhood, reveals the extent of his ambivalence. In 1936 Frances Byng-Stamper of the Contemporary Art Society for Wales implored him to attend the opening of the Eisteddfod exhibition in Fishguard.[35] 'I don't see myself doing so,' he wrote to Dorelia. '[J. B.] Manson [director of the Tate Gallery] is opening her show of Contemporary Welsh Art. It all makes me rather sick' (NLW MS 22778D, f. 137, [20 July 1936]). His antipathy towards Manson clearly overrode any feeling towards Wales or even his native Pembrokeshire, and the reference to *'her* show' [my italics] indicates a concern to distance himself from the proceedings. Ironically, the exhibition from which he was so anxious to disassociate himself included three pictures by Gwen John, which presumably met with his approval. These pictures were 'much admired', as their father reported in an enthusiastic letter to Gwen, having enjoyed the Eisteddfod 'exceedingly' (NLW MS 22306D, ff. 109^{r-v}).

But Augustus did take part in the judging of the Eisteddfod art competitions, although he went visiting Caitlin and Dylan Thomas instead of spending time at the Eisteddfod itself. 'The Works of Art sent up seemed to have been dug out of some mouldy Victorian sea-side lodging house. There was only one which could be called a real painting,' he complained, but the fact that he did not bother to identify the artist of that one painting is more revealing of his own indifference than of the true state of indigenous Welsh art.[36] He dismissed the work of Alfred Janes, whom he met with the Thomases, as 'very dissapointing [sic] being really rotten' (NLW MS 22778D, f. 136^v). The fact that he fails to remember Janes's name correctly may suggest that he had not studied the pictures with any great care.[37]

His lack of understanding of the ground from which so many of his compatriot artists sprang demonstrates that Augustus was an outsider to Wales and to the art world within Wales, and the lack of any informed empathy is evident from his comments on the South Wales painter Evan Walters. At the Swansea Eisteddfod in 1926 John had praised Walters warmly, calling one of his pictures 'damn good'.[38] But by the time of Walters's death in March 1951 his attitude had changed. Writing to David Bell in July that same year, he admitted that he did not know Walters well, 'having only met him two or three times in London for little more than a few minutes' (NLW MS 22779E, f. 70, transcript). The Swansea Eisteddfod now totally forgotten, he proceeds to damn him with faint praise. He concedes that the exhibition which Walters had at Dorothy Warren's gallery in Mayfair was 'interesting' but deplores his quiet refusal to take John's advice to 'go to paint in Provence and so develop a colour sense'. Walters, he concludes dismissively, 'did not do so but always drifted back to South Wales where colour is apparently taboo or non-existent'.

Such disparaging remarks about South Wales are not uncommon, but must be set in their immediate context and in that of John's own conflicting feelings towards his native country. They may not necessarily represent an opinion held with conviction or consistency; rather they may reflect his feelings at a specific moment or a wish to present a particular persona to a particular correspondent.

If Augustus at times appears unsympathetic to indigenous Welsh artists such as Evan Walters and later Alfred Janes, he was yet more negative in his remarks about other sections of the community in Wales. His friendship with Lord Howard de Walden, an influential patron of the arts in Wales, led to Augustus visiting Cardiff shortly before the First World War to see Welsh plays staged by Howard de Walden and written by the colourful and ambiguous Colonel Arthur Vaughan, alias Owen Rhoscomyl, author of a romanticised but influential work entitled *Flamebearers of Welsh History* (1905). The plays went well, he wrote to Dorelia, but Captain Vaughan 'is a dirty sucker', whilst the players themselves are 'people out of the coalmines. They will be biting each other's ears soon' (NLW MS 22777D, f. 44). It may be that there was an element of playing to the gallery in these words: they were addressed to Dorelia who — unlike Ida Nettleship — seems to have evinced little interest in Wales, and he may have been distancing himself from conventional images of the Welsh people. Nonetheless, he claimed Welshness when it suited him, even in clichéd terms, such as boasting bombastically that 'My Father kept everything dark, but I had an uncle descended from Owen Glyndwr' (NLW MS 22775C, f. 3^v).[39] At bottom, however, Augustus John's papers suggest that he had little genuine contact with the country and its people and that for him it remained a place to visit, for its visual appeal to the artist in him and for the adulation that he received from the artistic establishment. It is striking that on his visits to Wales we find him accompanied — with the honourable exception of J. D. Innes — by outsiders, those with tenuous claims to be Welsh, or those with a passing interest in Wales. Those referred to in his letters include Howard de Walden, John Sampson, the composer Josef Holbrooke, and artists such as Derwent Lees and Sidney Sime. His ambivalence towards Wales was surely not unconnected with his difficult childhood and relationship with his father after his mother's early death. For Augustus, as for Gwen John, any nostalgia for Wales was for the coast and countryside of Pembrokeshire, which acted as a visual stimulus and a means of escape from the repressive atmosphere of home. His feelings are neatly summed up in a letter written to Michel Salaman during a stay in Newquay, on the Cardiganshire coast, in August 1901: 'This place is beginning to bore me — charming as it is. I ... shall be glad to get to Liverpool again' (NLW MS 14928D, f. 47). Wales was picturesque but best taken in small doses.

His attitude to Ireland and the Irish seems to have been similar, judging by his letters to Dorelia whilst staying there. His visits to County Galway in 1912 and 1915 produced a few enthusiastic generalisations about the countryside, such as his description of Renvyle as 'a most marvellous place' (NLW MS 22777D, f. 86), but on the whole the letters home convey a sense of irritation with his hosts and sitters. George Bernard Shaw he describes as 'a ridiculous vain object in knickerbockers' and Lady Gregory is 'just like Queen V[ictoria] only uglier' (ibid, ff. 80^{r-v}). This peevishness was perhaps brought on by the sedateness of the household at Coole Park: 'The Victorian oppression of this house is terrible', he complained. 'Nobody seems to smoke or drink here' (*ibid.*, ff. 80^v, 85), but familiarity too could turn admiration to contempt. Oliver St John Gogarty is first described as a 'great brick but such a mad hatter', but before long they had a row. 'He means well but he irritate[s] me', he reported to Dorelia. The final, damning sentence on Gogarty was that he was 'an underbred beast' and 'bored me considerably' (*ibid.*, ff. 97^v-8, 101, 103). No doubt John's increasingly bilious comments arise partly from a sense of isolation, even loneliness and homesickness, for he longs for Dorelia to come over with the children to join him ('I wish to God you were here'), even though, he adds gloomily, she would probably hate it there (*ibid.*, ff. 86-9).

This sense of isolation, which can often be discerned in Augustus John's letters, was perhaps inevitable in a man who, despite having a foot in many social and cultural contexts, never truly belonged to any one of them, and always saw them through the eyes of an outsider. Having once escaped from the oppressive atmosphere of his home in Tenby, he could never fully re-establish himself as a Welshman, even had he wished to do so, and it is noticeable that he found most attractive those communities which were as different as possible to the society in which he had grown up. The Gypsies attracted him because they were colourful and lived on the margins of society, although the fact that he was introduced to their world by John Sampson, who combined a delight in their company with a rigorous scholarly approach to studying their language and culture, encouraged him to fit his enthusiasm into a respectable intellectual framework, including contributing to the *Journal* of the Gypsy Lore Society. Nonetheless, it is much to his credit that in later life, when his days of living out the fantasy of travelling the lanes in a gypsy caravan were far behind him, he remained an active member of the Gypsy Lore Society, as witness the important series of letters from Dora Yates and other officers of the Society, of which he was made President in 1937.[40] He also maintained contact with the gypsies themselves, such as Cliff Lee, who camped in John's grounds at Fryern Court in 1959 and sat for his portrait (NLW MS 22787D, f. 100).[41] Lee wrote to thank Augustus afterwards (NLW MS 22783D, f. 15), which may seem unexpected from a gypsy, but even Dora Yates found Lee's 'breadth of reading and intellectual interests amazing' (NLW 22787D, f. 100). But this is not the only example of a gypsy writing to Augustus, for his papers also include two letters, in execrable French and Spanish, from the gypsy guitarist Fabian de Castro (NLW MS 22780E, ff. 11-14^v, *c.* 1909-10), and one letter, in English (NLW MS 22781D, ff. 70-1, 25 September 1932), survives from Rosie Griffiths, one of the last Welsh Romani-speakers, whose fatal throat cancer tragically prevented Dora Yates from recording her speech for posterity (NLW MS 22787D, ff. 72-3).[42]

Augustus John's interest in the gypsies brought him quite by chance into contact with another marginalised people, the Occitan speakers of southern France, for it was while he was searching for, and finding, gypsies in the region of Arles in January 1910 that a missed train led to his meeting a 'superb fellow', called Alphonse Brioule. It was Brioule, who had just finished writing a letter in his native Occitan to the poet Mistral, who introduced John to their culture. John reported excitedly to Dorelia how he had sketched Brioule, been invited to his house to see his 'seven fine Provençal children', and been taken by him to visit Mistral himself (NLW MS 22776D, ff. 107-10). Mistral refused to sit for his portrait, but Augustus included a sketch of him in his letter to Dorelia (*ibid.* f. 109^v, see Plate IX).

From gypsies to Irish girls to Occitan poets, what attracted Augustus was any group that existed outside — and in spite of — an increasingly uniform metropolitan culture. Yet, ironically, he himself depended on that culture for commissions and sales, however great his avowed distaste for it. From time to time he might escape to those exotic but increasingly disempowered communities, but could never be more than a visitor from outside. Within them, moreover, he would always be associated with that metropolitan society from which he wished to dissociate himself, at least temporarily. Nevertheless, he made admirable use of his social contacts with the famous and influential to help disadvantaged groups and individuals. One of the earliest examples is his intervention with David Lloyd George, via the latter's secretary and mistress,

Frances Stevenson, on behalf of the Polish artist Albert Lipczinski, whom John had known in Liverpool. On receiving news from John Sampson that Lipczinski had been arrested and taken to an internment camp in the Isle of Man (NLW MS 22785D, f. 24, 10 January 1919), Augustus, then in Paris working at portraits of the delegates to the European Peace Conference, lost no time in writing to Miss Stevenson, whom he already knew, most fortunately, through Lady Tredegar, mother of the eccentric Evan Morgan. Although Frances Stevenson's replies appear to be lost, his letters to her (NLW MS 21570E) had the desired effect, for a relieved letter from Sampson proves that by early February he had succeeded and the artist had been allowed to return home (NLW MS 22785D, ff. 25-6).

Similarly, in his later years Augustus John often used his influence to help gypsies in difficulties when they found themselves increasingly unwelcome at their traditional stopping places. After many years of painting portraits of politicians from David Lloyd George to Ramsay MacDonald, he was well placed to be heard in the corridors of power, and a forceful letter from him to the *Times* could lead to questions being asked in Parliament (NLW MSS 22781D, ff. 138-41, 1955-7, and 22787D, ff. 24-31, 1950). His campaign against the harrassment of gypsies continued unabated until his death, as a letter, dated 18 August 1961, from the novelist Barbara Cartland, then a Hertfordshire county councillor, shows (NLW MS 22779E, f. 140).

His concern for social justice was not new, however. Writing to Dorelia in 1913 he spoke warmly of the trade union leader Jim Larkin, then visiting London to intervene in an industrial dispute (NLW MS 22777D, f. 29^v). That he was also prepared to make both a public and practical stand is evident in his working with British Anarchists in 1946 to alleviate the situation of Spanish internees in Chorley, who had already suffered in German camps, a campaign in which Gerald Brenan was also involved (NLW MS 22779E, ff. 78-9, 80, 91-2). Even in his eighty-third year Augustus was still in contact with the Anarchist movement, and was invited to an 'Anarchist Ball ... a rather jazzy affair', to celebrate the seventy-fifth anniversary of the Freedom Press. The writer notes with awe that Augustus had known the Press's founder, Peter Kropotkin (NLW MS 22780E, f. 134, 13 October 1961).

Although these were causes to which he had become attached in his younger days, in his old age he embraced newer political issues. These included the campaign for the abolition of capital punishment, which brought him letters from the publisher Victor Gollancz (NLW MS 22781D, ff. 31-2) and the MP Montgomery Hyde (*ibid.*, ff. 138-9, 1955), and nuclear disarmament, where he found himself allied not only with the Mexican artist, Diego Rivera (NLW MS 22784D, ff. 119-20, 1957) and the English philosopher, Bertrand Russell (NLW

MS 22784D, f. 158, 1960), who successfully urged him to join the Committee of 100, but also his own son, David. David John's letters from this period, recounting his own arrest and brief imprisonment after an anti-nuclear demonstration in Trafalgar Square, provide a touching antidote to the usual image of Augustus John and his sons failing to communicate across a widening gap of misunderstanding (NLW MS 22782D, ff. 15-17, September-October 1961).

Although Augustus John's prominence brought him into contact with a wide range of well-known artists, writers, musicians, politicians and others, and these social contacts are reflected in his correspondence, the archive also shows the less glamorous side of his fame, for it demonstrates how it constantly exposed him to unsolicited letters from people anxious to gain his support. These include potential models, like the Myrtle Ogilvy who wrote to him in 1929 offering to sit for him (NLW MS 22784D, ff. 21-2), as well as requests for charitable donations, such as that from Felix Aprahamian asking for a contribution to a commemorative concert for the Polish musician Jan Sliwinski (NLW MS 22779E, f. 22, 1950), or one from the Cabdrivers' Benevolent Association (NLW MS 22786D, f. 66). Others seek his approval of their own or their relatives' paintings (e.g. NLW MSS 22780E, f. 16, 141^v-2^v, 22785D, ff. 73-5). Impoverished artists, such as Ulrica Forbes[43] and Phelan Gibb, wrote hoping to wring from him money as well as sympathy (NLW MSS 22780E, f. 99, 22781D, ff. 7-8^v). In these two instances his response is not recorded, but at times there is concrete evidence of John's generosity, notably to the artist and writer, Alexander Stewart Gray, whose letters reveal that he received considerable financial support from him (NLW MS 22781D, ff. 41-4). Similarly there are hopeful letters from obscure societies, such as the Literary and Debating Society of the South Wiltshire Secondary School for Girls at Salisbury, inviting him to address them (*ibid.*, ff. 71-2, 1929). He also received letters from eccentrics, such as a man asking Augustus to paint the portrait of his dog ('I could bring him to see you at any time', NLW MS 22787D, f. 43), a young woman recently released from Holloway Prison (NLW MS 22783D, ff. 46-9), a lady anxious to foist onto him a large gold-leaf picture-frame (NLW MS 22782D, f. 7), and a host of autograph hunters (e.g. NLW MSS 22779E, ff. 40-2, 1952, 22785D, f. 131). And although letters from short-term girlfriends are so conspicuously absent that one can only conclude that they were destroyed, whether immediately or subsequently, there are a few exceptions. One of them, from a girl in Galway, who signs herself 'Katie with Songs' is touching in its innocence, recalling 'the fun we used to have in the Bar', and wishing he was not married (NLW MS 22782D, f. 139).

Some light is naturally thrown by his papers on Augustus John's relationships with members of his own family. The early years of his marriage to Ida, his growing love for Dorelia and the reaction to this of his sister Gwen are well-documented, since all parties concerned seem to have taken care to preserve each other's letters from this eventful period of their lives. Those from Ida and Dorelia which were kept by Gwen John, and which I have discussed elsewhere,[44] are complemented by the numerous groups now forming part of the National Library's Augustus John Papers. Apart from five letters from Gwen John to Dorelia (NLW MSS 22789D, ff. 58-63^v, [1904-5], 22799D, f. 35, [1904]), these include three remarkable series of letters from Ida, from as early as the 1880s to her death in March 1907 after the birth of her fifth child, Henry (NLW MSS 22788C, 22789D, ff. 64-81^v, and 22798B). They are addressed to various correspondents, including her mother and sisters, Dorelia, and friends from schooldays and from the Slade, the latter including fourteen letters to Michel Salaman (NLW MS 22788C, ff. 57-81^v, 1898-1903), to whose brother Clement she had been briefly engaged. She had evidently been a keen and lively letter-writer even when very young, for the earliest example is addressed to her newborn sister Ursula (NLW MS 22798B, ff. 75-6^v). After her marriage and increasing unhappiness, isolated from her old friends partly by the regular arrival of yet another child, partly by the disapproval in some quarters of her *ménage-à-trois* with Augustus and Dorelia, and later simply by the removal of the *ménage* to Paris, she clearly relied increasingly on letters as a means of keeping in touch with friends and family. The way in which she manages to write philosophical, even cheerful letters, often with jokes at her own expense, in the middle of a chaos of sick or squabbling children and maids, suggests that keeping up her correspondence may have helped her to cope. Taken with the harrowing sequence in which her mother, Ada Nettleship, and her sister, Ethel, record day by day Ida's gradual sinking into death (NLW MS 22799D, ff. 36-47^v, March 1907), they provide a very moving record of her short but intensely-lived life, and document almost from month to month the shift from the hopeful, ambitious young woman artist, to the young wife and mother, struggling to come to terms at first with the impossibility of continuing her artistic career and then the difficulties of her marriage, especially after the advent of Dorelia. Some hint of her artistic style is provided by the rough sketches with which she illustrated the earliest letters to her women friends and sisters, including two nudes (NLW MS 22798B, f. 88^{r-v}, see Plate XII).

If Augustus, like other members of the John and Nettleship families, deliberately preserved as many letters from Ida as possible, it is remarkable how few of those which Gwen John must have written to him survive. Even allowing that she may not have written very often to him, the twenty-seven letters from Augustus, dating from 1904 to 1938, that she kept contain references to letters he has received from her but which do not appear to have survived (NLW MS 22305D, ff. 96-147^v).[45] Only five letters from Gwen to Augustus John are found amongst his papers, and these cover only the years from about 1910 to 1925, with no sign of letters from before the death of Ida in 1907 or immediately after. These five letters are supplemented by five others, written in 1914 and 1925-6, acquired separately by the National Library (NLW MS 22155B, ff. 9-12), but the total still remains very small, and a small proportion of what must have once existed. Similarly, the archive includes only five letters from Gwen to Dorelia, all of them, however, from the critical period of 1904-5 when Dorelia left Gwen John in Paris to live in Belgium with a young artist and was then finally persuaded to return to Augustus (NLW MSS 22789D, ff. 58-63^v, 22799D, f. 35). Again it appears that letters relating to these events were carefully preserved despite periods when Augustus and Dorelia had no long-term address. Gwen's letters to Augustus (NLW MS 22782D, ff. 29-34) are fairly typical, asking him to send her a bottle of Sanatogen tonic wine to help her over her 'funeste fatigue', or to make arrangements for a trunkful of her possessions to be sent over, but they also include brief references to the progress of her work. Writing in 1925, for example, after the death of her patron John Quinn the previous year, she reports that she is still struggling to finish the third painting she owed his estate. Later that same year she seems deeply and happily engrossed in her painting, for she puts off an invitation to visit because she is now doing 'some little drawings that interest me'. Her letters are at times somewhat impersonal in style, but with a few touches of genuine affection and pleasure, when she thanks him for his 'gentle solicitude', for example, or for the gift of a pair of earrings: 'My ears are pierced but I thought the time for ear[-r]ings was over for me. But these are so lovely I must wear them' (*ibid.*, ff. 29, 34).

As we have already noted, remarkably few letters from Dorelia are included in the archive: only eight, written between 1907 and 1938 (NLW MS 22783D, ff. 110-23). This contrasts starkly with over 250 from Augustus which Dorelia kept, and it is tempting to suppose that Dorelia kept his letters to her partly with an eye on posterity. It is striking, however, that the earliest surviving letters from Dorelia were kept by other people, including Gwen John (NLW MS 22308D, ff. 8-13, five items, written *c*. 1903-1906)[46] and John Sampson (NLW MS 21459E, ff. 91-7^v, three items, in Romani, *c*. 1903). It appears that Augustus made no conscious attempts to keep her letters and that those that have survived did so by chance. Similarly, only two letters from his sister Winifred are found among his papers. One of them, dated 3 January 1906, is extremely lively, containing not only personal news but amusing comments on other people, which may account for its survival (NLW MS 22782D, ff. 121-4^v). She fantasises about their evangelical

Aunt Rose camping in the Rocky Mountains and getting 'shot for a ferr[e]t' and makes unflattering comments about John Sampson, whose legs, she declares *'couldn't* get fatter without exploding'. The only other letter, dated 3 March 1956, is an intense plea to Augustus not to go ahead with his idea of writing a biography of Gwen John: 'There is no one in the world who would be more averse to having their private life made public', she wrote, adding that their brother Thornton agrees with her. 'Please be truly great and have mercy', she concludes (*ibid.*, f.125^{r-v}). Whether or not Augustus was moved by this letter, he never wrote the biography.[47] Winifred's claim in this letter that she knew Gwen better than anyone else may have some foundation, for it is clear from the sisters' correspondence that Gwen confided in Winifred more than she did to most people.[48]

The two surviving letters from Winifred to Augustus provide little evidence for such a close relationship between them, and the same is true of the letters from Thornton John. Six of his letters to Augustus are included in the archive (NLW MS 22782D, ff. 110-20), dated 1948-59, their late dates suggesting that they were simply never thrown away rather than being kept deliberately. Most of Thornton's letters are concerned with his own life in Canada, although the earliest suggests a possible epitaph for their father's gravestone, 'With long life I shall satisfy him and show him my salvation', a suggestion which Augustus in fact accepted. As the elder brother he writes in a teasingly unimpressed vein about Augustus's award of the freedom of the Borough of Tenby in 1959. 'It means simply civic amour propre, something good to drink. A few little speeches and jokes, a write-up in the papers', he warns, adding that Augustus will have to get a new suit (*ibid.*, f. 120).

In contrast to the rather thin coverage of letters from his brother and sisters, the archive includes a surprisingly large number of letters to Augustus from his sons, notably David, Edwin, Henry, Robin and Romilly. There are none from his daughters, Poppet and Vivien, although neither was averse to letter-writing, as witness the two series from them to their brother Edwin, now in the Gwen John archive (NLW MS 22312D, ff. 85-101^v, 105-78). Since Henry, the last of Ida's sons, was drowned at the age of twenty-eight, it is perhaps understandable that Augustus kept a number of his letters (NLW MS 22782D, ff. 35-54^v, 1924-*c.*1932). This group stands out because of the confidence which Henry displays in addressing his father, particularly on intellectual and religious matters. This may be accounted for by his more stable and conventional upbringing amongst the Nettleships and his rigorous Catholic education, but also perhaps by the fact that he had been brought up apart from the rest of the family and had been exposed far less to his father's moods. It is significant that his brother Caspar, who decided fairly early that his future career lay in the disciplined life of the Navy, seems to have coped better with his father than did the other sons who led a more unstructured existence.[49] Augustus's letters to Caspar, now included in the archive, albeit from the last, perhaps more mellow decade of his life, are generally approving and adopt a 'man to man' style (NLW MS 22775C, ff. 2-55^v, 1950-61), in stark contrast to his bullying letters to Edwin, whom he treats more as a schoolboy than as a man in his thirties and forties (NLW MS 22312D, ff. 10-77, 1938-56).[50] Fortunately the survival of at least part of the other side of the correspondence amongst Augustus's papers means that Edwin's side of the story can now be heard (NLW MS 22782D, ff. 18-25^v, 1935-61). A brief reference in a single surviving letter from Augustus to Henry, in which he declares that he likes Edwin 'immensely' now that 'he has become a tall, happy fellow full of confidence, humour and character', and 'from all accounts a nut at boxing in Paris' (NLW MS 22775C, ff. 56^v), hints that he was indeed proud of his sons but that his relationships with them as adults were bedevilled by lack of communication leading to constant misunderstandings. The letters from David, Robin and Romilly, although they survive only in small numbers and cannot be taken as representative, reveal their attempts to find different strategies for coping with their father, by turns striving to find some common ground, to smooth over tensions and to reassure him that they are achieving something in their lives (NLW MS 22782D, ff. 8-17, 96-108^v).

* * * * *

As the foregoing account suggests, the vast bulk of the Augustus John archive consists of correspondence. Apart from the four sketchbooks discussed above (p. 5), other papers of the artist include drafts of prose and light verse by him (NLW MSS 22795-6). Of these the prose consists mainly of drafts of autobiographical writings published in *Chiaroscuro* in 1952 and *Finishing Touches* in 1964, some chapters having previously appeared in *Horizon* and *The Sunday Times*.[51] In writing about his life, Augustus was evidently concerned to project a particular image of himself and preoccupied with writing in a particular style, which leads to considerable obfuscation and tempts the reader to speculative reading between the lines. The chief interest of the drafts lies in the constant revisions and corrections to which he subjected them, revealing his unwillingness or incapacity to consider any draft definitive. Two small groups of papers in NLW MSS 22797D and 22800E, immediately postdating his death, document his memorial service and the unveiling of his memorial statue at Fordingbridge. Not surprisingly, such postmortem material reveals more about formal, public perceptions of the deceased than about the man himself.

The papers of Augustus John are naturally closely related to those of his sister, Gwen, not only because of the family ties which maintained some level of contact between them throughout their lives, but also because as artists and individuals they shared certain preoccupations, friendships and experiences. Their respective archives, however, present a number of contrasts. In terms of bulk, the Augustus John papers held at the National Library of Wales far exceed those of Gwen John, although his couple of hundred letters to Dorelia pale into insignificance when set against the couple of thousand letters from Gwen to Auguste Rodin preserved at the Musée Rodin in Paris.[52] But the difference in the content of their respective archives, unrepresentative as haphazard survival may make them, is nonetheless striking.

Although both brother and sister often expressed themselves through both words and visual images, often on the same page, in Gwen's case this was done for personal use only, in notebooks and on scraps of paper, whilst the examples in Augustus's papers are confined to letters and thus intended to entertain other people. The fact that letters to Augustus survive in far greater profusion and from a far greater variety of correspondents means also that his life is not so much reflected in his papers as refracted from countless different directions. Furthermore, whereas a significant proportion of the papers found in Gwen John's rooms at her death is made up of diaries, notebooks and personal jottings of all kinds, in which she notes ideas for pictures, and records and analyses, with pitiless self-knowledge, her feelings and aspirations, no such material survives among her brother's papers. Even his light verse was written for an audience of family and friends, and his autobiographical writings were commissioned for publication. In Gwen John's case the focus of her life narrows and becomes increasingly inward as time goes on, and the outer world gradually loses interest for her. The papers of Augustus, in contrast, perhaps conceal as much as they reveal, for they build up an impression of a man preoccupied with presenting to his own circle and to the outside world a particular image, or set of images, even if those images were not always of his own making but imposed on him by others. The survival of his substantial archive enables that process of image-making to continue.

1   Ceridwen Lloyd-Morgan, *Gwen John Papers at the National Library of Wales* (2nd ed., Aberystwyth, 1995).
2   The standard biography has been Michael Holroyd, *Augustus John* (2 vols, London, 1974); a new biography by Holroyd is to be published in 1996.
3   See Daniel Huws, 'Some Letters of Augustus John', *National Library of Wales Journal*, xv (1967-8), 236, plates xv.7-8. Although only ten letters survive from John to Ursula Tyrwhitt, and the bulk of these are from the turn of the century, they kept in touch, however infrequently, all their lives, for the the last letter is dated 1958. John's letters to Dorelia also mention her visiting him in London in 1912 (NLW MS 27777D, f. 9).
4   The original letters were part of the major archive sold at Sotheby's in 1979 (see below, p.4), but when that archive was sold to the Library in 1989 they were retained by the seller, who provided photocopies of the letters from John Sampson, Dora Yates and other members of the Gypsy Lore Society. Many of these letters, like those from John to Sampson, are written wholly or partly in Romani. A synopsis of the content of each is provided in the *Catalogue of Augustus John Papers*, 167-71.
5   It is possible, however, that John felt that their relationship was one-sided in this respect, for in a letter probably written in 1904 he reproaches Sampson: 'I wish you'd only treat me more as a confidante' (NLW MS 21489E, f. 12).
6   See NLW *Catalogue of Gwen John Papers* (1988) and Ceridwen Lloyd-Morgan, *Gwen John Papers at the National Library of Wales*.
7   See introduction to *Catalogue of Augustus John Papers*, and the Library's *Annual Report, 1987-88*, 61, *1988-89*, 66.
8   Further details of the location of manuscript holdings are given by Michael Holroyd in his new biography of Augustus John (1996).
9   In 1974 the National Museum of Wales acquired an important group of over a thousand drawings and rough sketches together with over a hundred unfinished or rejected paintings, representing the remainder of what had been left in Augustus John's studios at his death, after auction sales of selected material at Christie's in 1962 and 1963. See A. D. Fraser Jenkins, *Augustus John. Studies for Compositions* (Cardiff, 1978), and, for a more recent account of the Museum's holdings, Mark L. Evans, *Portraits by Augustus John. Family, Friends and the Famous* (Cardiff, 1988). A small but interesting collection of drawings and paintings by Augustus (and Gwen) John is also held at the Castle Museum, Tenby.
10 For further details of these and other portraits by Augustus John held at the National Library, see appendix, pp.34-5.
11 See Plate XI. These sketches may be compared in subject and style with nos 69-77 in A. D. Fraser Jenkins, *Augustus John. Studies for Compositions*.
12 Compare the caricature of Stresemann at the National Museum of Wales: see Mark L. Evans, *Portraits by Augustus John*, 47, plate 35.
13 Alicia Gower Jones was headmistress of Grove Park Girls' School, Wrexham, and money had been raised by her friends and colleagues to commission her portrait. A series of letters to her from Augustus survives (Miss Olive Mary Jones Bequest at NLW, see appendix, p.34), as do the three drawings which he mentions in the letter to Dorelia (now also at NLW, see appendix, p.34).
14 The book to which Joyce refers was presumably Herbert Hughes (ed.), *The Joyce Book* (London, 1933), which contained musical settings by various composers for Joyce's *Pomes Penyeach*.
15 For letters from Craster about his own portait, see NLW MS 22779E, ff. 180-1.
16 For letters from Frida Strindberg, [?1911-14] see NLW MS 22785D, ff. 140-53^v; for draft letters from Augustus John to her, [?1911], see NLW MS 22775C, ff. 99-102.

17 For two letters from Kennerley to Augustus John, see NLW MS 22782D, ff. 151-3^v.
18 NLW MS 22309C, ff. 1-133, 1911-24, see *Catalogue of Gwen John Papers*, 46-51.
19 See Alison Thomas, *Portraits of Women. Gwen John and her Forgotten Contemporaries* (Cambridge, 1994), 166-77.
20 See also Jane Hill, *The Art of Dora Carrington* (London, 1994), 127.
21 On these designs, see Holroyd, i, 324-5, ii, 35, and A. D. Fraser Jenkins, *Augustus John. Studies for Compositions* (not paginated).
22 See Holroyd, ii, 174.
23 According to Frances Byng-Stamper of CASW, John shared Morris's concern for the distressed areas of South Wales in the 1930s and was anxious to focus at least some of the movement's activities in such places. See *Contemporary Art Society for Wales. 50th Anniversary Exhibition Catalogue* (Cardiff, 1987), 6.
24 See below, pp.17-18.
25 Disappointingly, the papers of Mrs Coombe Tennant held at the National Library of Wales contain no letters from Augustus John. See typescript *Schedule of Manuscripts ... of the late Mrs Winifred Coombe Tennant* (1958).
26 Philip Heseltine often stayed at his mother's home at Cefnbryn-talch, Abermule, Montgomeryshire; one letter from him to John survives (NLW MS 22781D, f. 110, 1930), and ten letters from John to Heseltine (NLW MS 18909D, 1920-9). Augustus contributed the foreword to Cecil Gray, *Peter Warlock. A Memoir of Philip Heseltine* (London, 1934). Josef Holbrooke benefited greatly from the patronage of Howard de Walden, who commissioned from him extravagant orchestral and operatic works of Welsh inspiration. Holbrooke stayed in Wales on various occasions, with the Howard de Waldens at Chirk, and at Nant-ddu, Cwm Prysor, and Llwynythyl [*recte* Llwynithel], Tanygrisiau, with Augustus John and others. See Holroyd, ii, 33, 36. For letters between John and Holbrooke see NLW MSS 22781D, ff. 116-19, 1951-7, and 23410C, ff.1-11; see also references in John's letters to Dorelia McNeill, e.g. NLW MS 22777D, ff. 12^v, 24, 44^v, and NLW MS 23410C, ff. 12-13.
27 See also Mark L. Evans, *Portraits by Augustus John*, 38-9, plates 22-3, and Holroyd, ii, 31-3.
28 See also Ceridwen Lloyd-Morgan, *Gwen John Papers at the National Library of Wales*, 4-6, and 'Cymry oddi cartref: hunaniaeth a hunanddelwedd rhai o arlunwyr yr 20fed ganrif', to appear in *Taliesin*, 97, (Spring 1997).
29 Although, as Sampson states in this same letter, the text had been sent to the Clarendon Press in 1917, the First World War delayed publication. In August 1919 Sampson complained to John that his 'unhappy book' was still like 'Mahomet's coffin, balanced between earth and heaven' (NLW MS 22785D, f. 27) and it did not finally appear until 1926. In the context of John's visits to Wales with Sampson it is tempting to speculate whether the artist ever met the respectable, chapel-going, Welsh novelist, Elena Puw Morgan (1900-73), who lived at Corwen and knew John Sampson, for she represents a bridge between the poles of Welsh life exemplified by the stuffiness of anglicised, middle-class Tenby on the one hand and the unfettered *joie de vivre* of the gypsies on the other. Her novel, *Nansi Lovell. Hunangofiant Hen Sipsi* (Aberystwyth, 1944), although no doubt inspired by M. Eileen Lyster's *The Gypsy Life of Betsy Wood* (London, 1926), draws on information gained directly from Sampson as well as personal contact with the Wood family of Romanis. See Marian Tomos, 'Bywyd a gwaith Elena Puw Morgan' (University of Wales MA thesis, Bangor, 1980).
30 Michael Holroyd, *Augustus John*, i, 8.
31 Cecily Langdale, *Gwen John* (New Haven & London, 1987), 4.
32 The note reads:'Gaer Duw egur y deall/Gaer Duw Rhydd olwg i'r Dall/Hwda my llaw/gyda my llun'. The use of capitals is as unorthodox as the spelling, although the latter (notably 'gaer' for 'gair' and 'egur' for 'egyr') might conceivably be construed as an attempt

to reproduce northern pronunciation. If so, this note could derive from one of his trips to North Wales with Sampson or J. D. Innes.

33 See A. D. Fraser Jenkins, *J. D. Innes at the National Museum of Wales* (Cardiff, 1975), and Eric Rowan, *Some Miraculous Promised Land. J. D. Innes, Augustus John and Derwent Lees in North Wales, 1910-13* (Llandudno, 1982).
34 See Papers of the Reverend R. J. Jones (at NLW), one letter, 1960, relating to the appointment of the chairman of the National Broadcasting Council for Wales.
35 Augustus had been present at the first meeting of CASW in May 1935. He agreed to select works for its first exhibition, whose success led to the decision to mount a further show at the National Eisteddfod in Fishguard in 1936. Mrs Byng-Stamper lived at Manorbier Castle in Pembrokeshire and it was understood that Augustus shared her commitment to the county. Augustus remained a member of the committee of CASW until his death, was elected its chairman in 1946 and its first president in 1960. See *Contemporary Art Society for Wales. 50th Anniversary Exhibition Catalogue*, 6, 10, 15.
36 The artist was presumably Dennis Jones of Birkenhead, since his was the winning picture. See Peter Lord, *Y Chwaer-Dduwies. Celf, Crefft a'r Eisteddfod* (Llandysul, 1992), 104.
37 See also Peter Lord, *Y Chwaer-Dduwies*, 101-4, and *Gwenllian. Essays on Visual Culture* (Llandysul, 1994), 136.
38 Peter Lord, *Y Chwaer-Dduwies*, 87-8, *Gwenllian*, 135.
39 It is worth noting his use here of the Welsh spelling of Glyndwr, rather than the anglicised Glendower.
40 For letters from Dora Yates see NLW MS 22787D, ff. 51-113, 1931-60; other groups relating to the GLS are those from H. J. Francis (NLW MS 22780E, ff. 107-28, 1952-9) and from R. A. Scott MacFie (NLW MS 22783D, ff. 66-84, 1910-32).
41 Clifford Lee, grandson of Ithel Lee who took part with Augustus John in the ceremony of scattering John Sampson's ashes in 1931, was apparently first introduced to the artist in 1959 by the gypsy scholar F. G. Huth: see NLW MS 22781D, f. 137.
42 See also Dora E. Yates, *My Gypsy Days. Recollections of a Romani Rawnie* (London, 1953), 112-13.
43 She died in 1960, see NLW MS 22781D, f. 105.
44 See Ceridwen Lloyd-Morgan, *Gwen John Papers at the National Library of Wales*, 11-12, 15-16.
45 See *Catalogue of Gwen John Papers*, 23-5.
46 See *Catalogue of Gwen John Papers*, 39. The same group includes some thirty-three others (ff. 14-56), from the years 1926-39, see *Catalogue*, 39-41.
47 It is not known whether Winifred had read Augustus's chapter on their sister in his volume of autobiography, *Chiaroscuro* which had been published four years earlier in 1952 (see Augustus John, *Autobiography* (London, 1975), 275-84), and which touches on Gwen John's strong emotional attachments. If Winifred had read it, she would have feared the worst.
48 See Ceridwen Lloyd-Morgan, *Gwen John Papers at the National Library of Wales*, 9-10.
49 See Rebecca John, *Caspar John* (London, 1987).
50 See *Catalogue of Gwen John Papers*, 62-5. Forty further letters from the same series were acquired in March 1996 and are now included in NLW MS 23508D.
51 See also NLW MSS 21570E, and 22775C, ff. 89-98, and NLW ex 1237/5.
52 See *Rodin, Whistler et la Muse* (Paris, 1995), published by the Musée Rodin to coincide with an exhibition focusing on the Whistler memorial, for which Gwen John was the model.

APPENDIX: SUMMARY OF HOLDINGS

This appendix summarises all holdings in the National Library of Wales with the exception of printed material.

AUGUSTUS JOHN PAPERS
For details see *Catalogue of Augustus John Papers*.

NLW MSS

22775C	LETTERS FROM AUGUSTUS JOHN, Jeanne Robert Foster — Frida Strindberg.
22776D	LETTERS FROM AUGUSTUS JOHN, Dorelia McNeill, [1903-?1911].
22777D	LETTERS FROM AUGUSTUS JOHN, Dorelia McNeill, [?1912-?1917].
22778D	LETTERS FROM AUGUSTUS JOHN, Dorelia McNeill, 191[8]-[1950].
22779E	LETTERS TO AUGUSTUS JOHN, Edward Austin Abbey Memorial Trust Fund — Nancy Cunard.
22780E	LETTERS TO AUGUSTUS JOHN, Adrian ?Daintrey — S. E. Furfie.
22781D	LETTERS TO AUGUSTUS JOHN, Marius Galeron — Scharmel Iris.
22782D	LETTERS TO AUGUSTUS JOHN, Alice James — Gonnoske Komai.
22783D	LETTERS TO AUGUSTUS JOHN, Henry Lamb — Ursula Nettleship.
22784D	LETTERS TO AUGUSTUS JOHN, Gordon Nettleton — John Russell.
22785D	LETTERS TO AUGUSTUS JOHN, Lord Salisbury — R. W. Symonds.
22786D	LETTERS TO AUGUSTUS JOHN, Arthur Symons — H. Vollot.
22787D	LETTERS TO AUGUSTUS JOHN, C. G. Wainwright — Margaret Zogbaum; unidentified correspondents.
22788C	LETTERS TO IDA JOHN, Margaret Hinton — Michel Salaman.
22789D	LETTERS TO DORELIA McNEILL, Boris Anrep — Dora Yates.
22790D	MISCELLANEOUS LETTERS, mainly to and from members of the John and Nettleship families.
22791C	AUGUSTUS JOHN: SKETCH BOOK, [1908].
22792-4A	AUGUSTUS JOHN: SKETCH BOOKS, [mid 1920s].
22795C	Drafts of *Chiaroscuro*, [c. 1938-51].
22796E	Incomplete drafts of *Finishing Touches* and related prose; drafts of light verse.
22797D	MISCELLANEOUS PAPERS, 1930-?1973, including papers of the artist and relating to him.
22798B	LETTERS FROM IDA JOHN, Margaret Hinton — Brenda Seligman; unidentified correspondent.
22799D	CORRESPONDENCE OF NETTLESHIP & JOHN FAMILIES, 1899-1980.

22800E	NETTLESHIP & JOHN FAMILY PAPERS, c. 1908-67.
22801A	ARTHUR SYMONS: NOTEBOOK, c. 1909.
22802D	LIST OF AUGUSTUS JOHN PAPERS, by Ronald Hamand c. 1977.
22803D	INDEX to MS 22802D.

OTHER MANUSCRIPTS
NLW MSS

11067C	AUGUSTUS JOHN: APPRECIATION OF J. D. INNES, n.d.
14928D	LETTERS FROM AUGUSTUS JOHN, Michel Salaman, [1898-1955].
16098E	LETTER FROM AUGUSTUS JOHN (item 212), Mr Squire, [1909 x 14].
18909D	LETTERS FROM AUGUSTUS JOHN, Mrs Goeritz, Ruth King and Philip Heseltine, 'Peter Warlock', 1920-54.
19645C	LETTERS FROM AUGUSTUS JOHN, Ursula Tyrwhitt, 1895-1958.
21459E	LETTERS FROM AUGUSTUS JOHN, John Sampson, 1902-[1927].
21482D	LETTERS FROM AUGUSTUS JOHN, various correspondents, including Robert Gregory, [c. 1908-9]-1936.
21570E	LETTERS FROM AUGUSTUS JOHN, various correspondents, including Dame Laura Knight and Frances Stevenson, 1913-54.
21585E	LETTERS FROM AUGUSTUS JOHN, John Davenport, 1938-61, with related articles and BBC script.
21622D	LETTERS FROM AUGUSTUS JOHN, Bapsy Pavry and Dr Pavry, 1932-53.
21698E	LETTER FROM AUGUSTUS JOHN (f. 64), Caitlin Macnamara, [1937].
21818E	LETTERS FROM AUGUSTUS JOHN, various correspondents [c. 1919]-1944.
21872D	LETTER FROM AUGUSTUS JOHN (f. 50), John Cowper Powys, 1958.
21980C	LETTERS FROM AUGUSTUS JOHN, Sean O'Casey and George Bilainkin, 1926-52.
22022C	LETTERS FROM AUGUSTUS JOHN, Villiers Bergne, 1941-58.
22022C	LETTER TO AUGUSTUS JOHN (f. 2), H. R. Alexander, 1941.
22155B	LETTERS TO AUGUSTUS JOHN (ff. 9-12), Gwen John, [1914-26]. (See *Catalogue of Gwen John Papers*, p. 82).
22305D	LETTERS FROM AUGUSTUS JOHN (ff. 96-147), Gwen John, 1904-38. (See *Catalogue of Gwen John Papers*, pp. 23-5).
22311D	LETTER FROM AUGUSTUS JOHN (f. 135), Dorelia McNeill, [1908]. (See *Catalogue of Gwen John Papers*, p. 60).
22312D	LETTERS FROM AUGUSTUS JOHN (ff. 10-77), Edwin John, 1938-

                56. (See *Catalogue of Gwen John Papers*, pp. 62-5).
22745D   LETTER FROM AUGUSTUS JOHN (f. 1), Keidrych Rhys, [1938].
23007E   LETTERS FROM AUGUSTUS JOHN (ff. 109-10), Ceri Richards, 1960.
23186E   LETTER FROM AUGUSTUS JOHN (f. 14), Port Talbot Forum, 1949.
23410C   LETTERS FROM AUGUSTUS JOHN, Josef Holbrooke, Charles Conder, Dorelia MacNeill, 1901-43.
23419D   LETTERS FROM AUGUSTUS JOHN (ff. 12-15), Keidrych Rhys, 1959.
23508D   LETTERS FROM AUGUSTUS JOHN, Edwin John, 1934-61.
23509E   JOHN FAMILY: MISCELLANEOUS PAPERS, 1931-72.
23510A   JOHN FAMILY PHOTOGRAPHS, [1880s-1920s].

OTHER COLLECTIONS AT NLW
NLW ex 1237: Printed and miscellaneous items, including reproductions of paintings and drawings by Augustus John.
NLW ex 1607: Miscellaneous papers relating to the John and Nettleship families.
Papers of the Rev. R. J. Jones, Cardiff: include a letter, 1960, from Augustus John.
Miss Olive Mary Jones Bequest, box 7: includes letters, 1944-58, from Augustus John to Miss Alicia Gower Jones.
Emlyn Williams Scrapbook II (1937-40): contains a letter, 1940, from Augustus John.
Dr Thomas Jones CH Collection, Class L, vol. 2, nos 29, 173: letters from Augustus John to Hugh Blaker and R. A. Maynard, 1926-7.
Gwyn Jones Papers, 41/242, 329, 334, 69/16: letters from Augustus John to Gwyn Jones, [1916x35], 1943-4.
Welsh Arts Council Archives, A/E/4-5, 30, 121, 380: papers relating to exhibitions of work by Augustus John (not to be consulted without written permission of the depositor).

PICTURES
(Department of Pictures and Maps)
PE 03846   Study of Gwen John [in fancy dress], bistre wash with crayon, *c.* 1900-1, 316 x 203 mm.
PB 06070   Portrait of a girl, black chalk, early 20th cent., 342 x 251 mm.
PB 04671   Portrait of David Lloyd George, oil on canvas, 1920, 646 x 470 mm.
PZ 03979   Portrait of Miss Alicia Gower Jones, pencil and crayon, 1944, 473 x 310 mm.
                The two other portraits, made during the same sittings, are now PB 08297 and PB 08298.

PE 04806   Portrait of John Stuart Corbett, oil on canvas, n.d. but pre 1921, 1030 x 900mm.

The Department of Pictures and Maps also holds a number of photographs of Augustus John and members of his family.

VIDEOCASSETTES
The Library's Sound and Moving Image Collection has the following video cassette, which can be viewed by appointment:

'Augustus and Gwen John; the Fire and the Fountain' (Miranda Films Videorecording, 1975).

Plate I. NLW MS 14928D, f.6.
Self-portrait.

Plate II. NLW MS 21459E, f.99.
Portrait of John Sampson.

Plate III. NLW MS 19645C, item 5.
Self-portrait.

Plate IV. NLW MS 19645C, item 3.
Self-portrait with donkey.

Plate V. NLW MS 19645C, item 7.
Self-portrait with Ambrose McEvoy.

Plate VI. NLW MS 19645C, item 2.
Wilson Steer's beard.

BRASSERIE WIELEMANS-CEUPPENS

Café Métropole
BRUXELLES

The time is nearly up - Ardor.
Gand is very near Bruges
I am to rejoin you on Tuesday
morning. So be it.
Do not let me go to the post
with no yellow card to bring away

Plate VII. NLW MS 22776D, f.32.
Self-portrait with Dorelia.

Plate VIII. NLW MS 22776D, ff.97ᵛ-98ʳ.
Chaloner Dowdall.

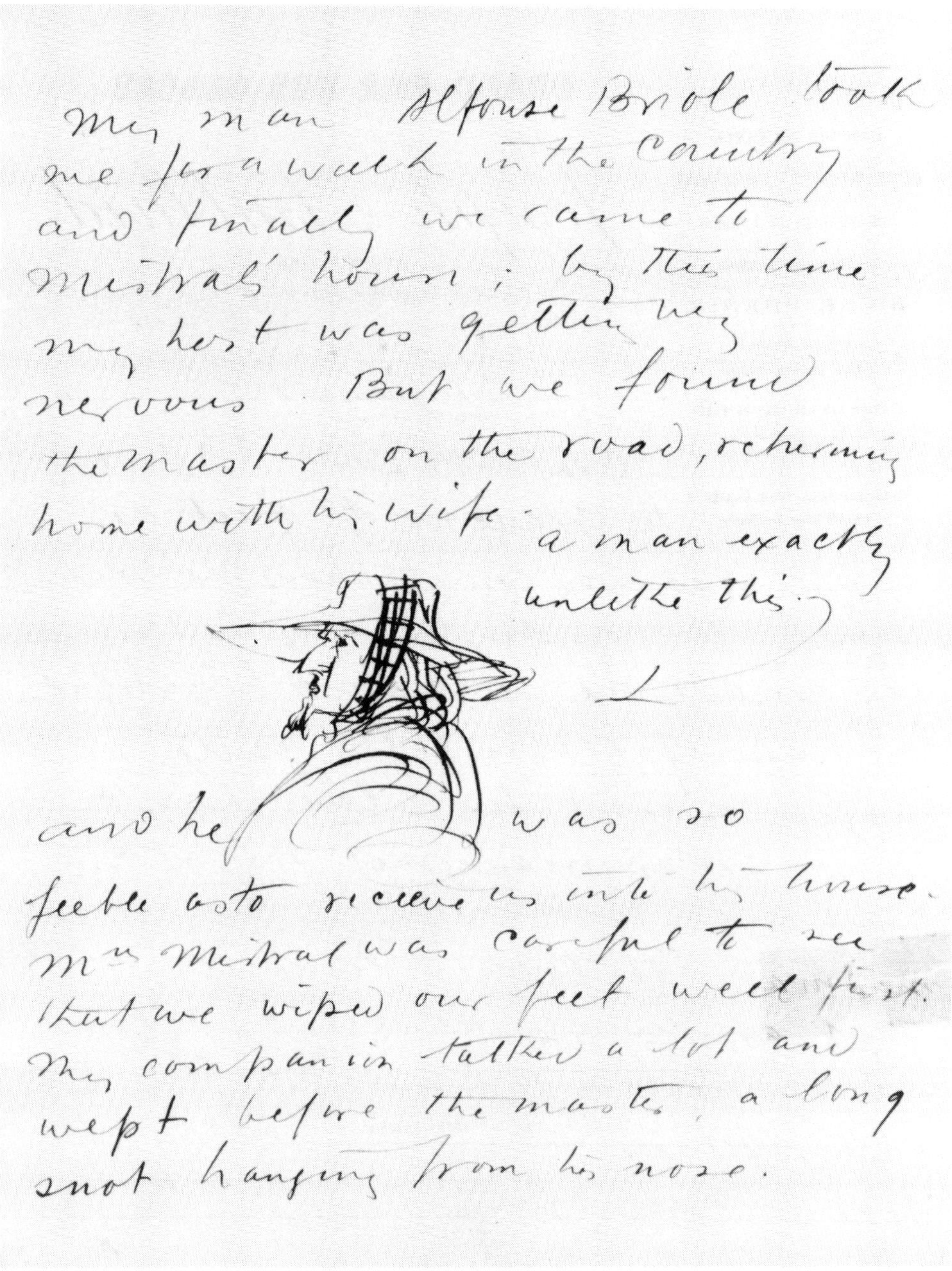

My man Alfonse Briole took me for a walk in the country and finally we came to Mistral's house; by this time my host was getting very nervous. But we found the master on the road, returning home with his wife. A man exactly unlike this, and he was so feeble as to receive us into his house. Mrs Mistral was careful to see that we wiped our feet well first. My companion talked a lot and wept before the master, a long snot hanging from his nose.

Plate IX. NLW MS 22776D, f.109ᵛ.
Frédéric Mistral.

manage not [to see?] much of them. Are the Schavies well? Kanwta ka čumera Mput.

Plate X. NLW MS 22776D, f.148ᵛ.
Self-portrait.

Plate XI. NLW MS 22791C, f.6.
Figure composition.

Plate XII. NLW MS 22798B, f.88^v.
Nude study by Ida Nettleship.